Paris

Germany

New York City

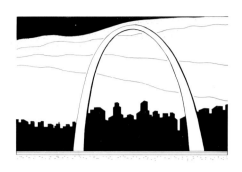
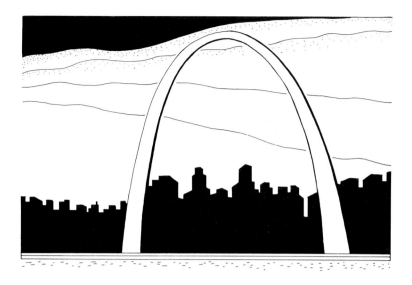

St. Louis

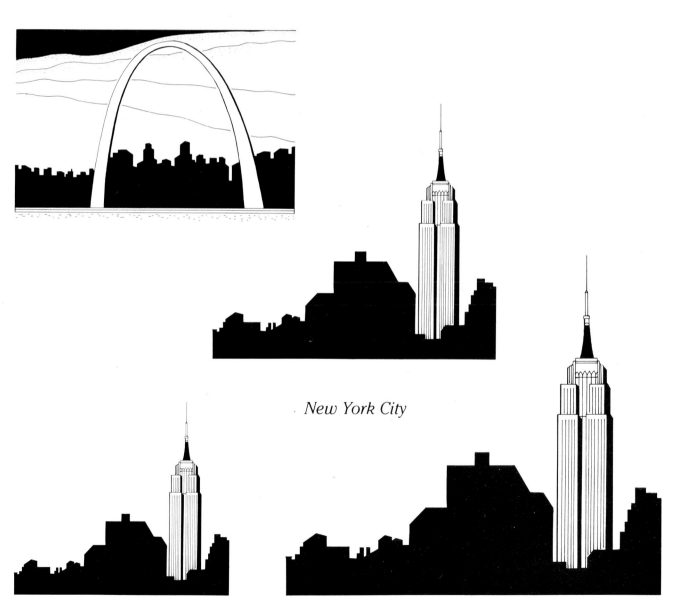

New York City

3

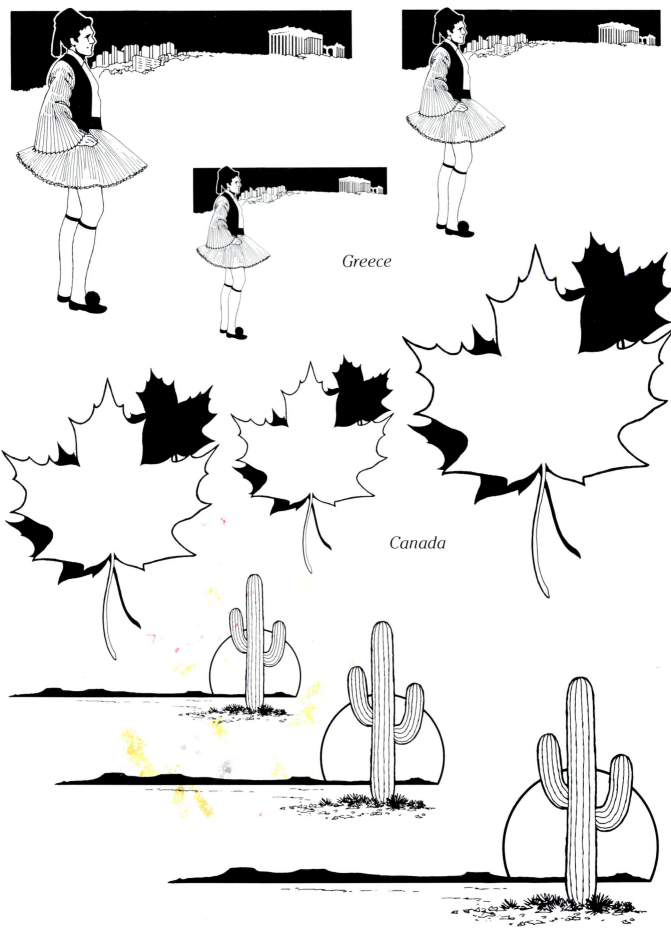

India

Moscow

Egypt

Ireland

San Francisco

New York City

Copenhagen

Japan   *Near East*

The Netherlands

India

Venice

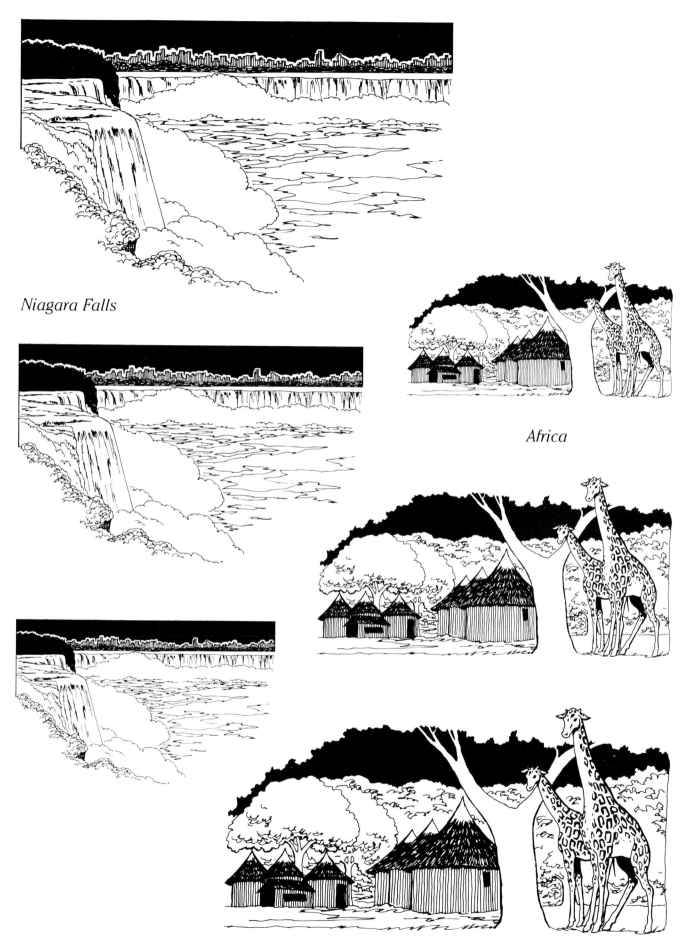

Niagara Falls

Africa

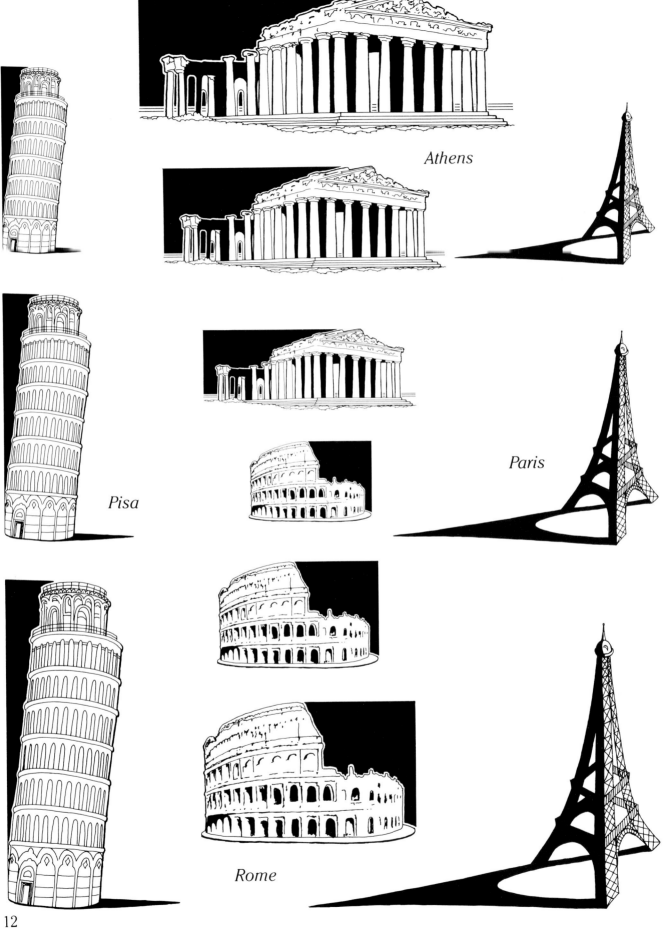

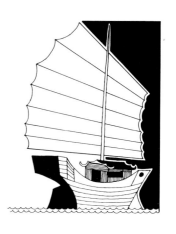

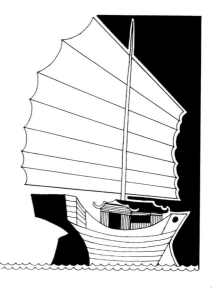

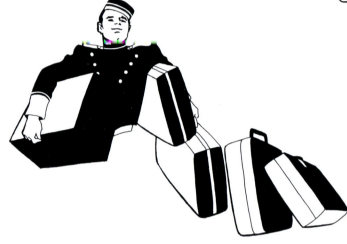

Mexico

Spain

Germany

Washington, D.C.

London

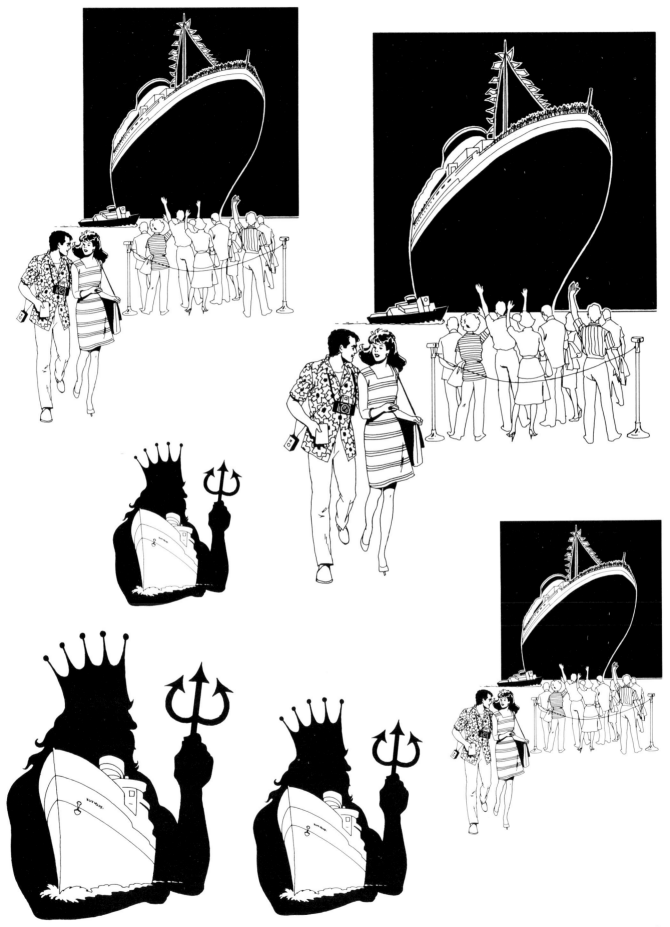

Paris

London

Rome

London

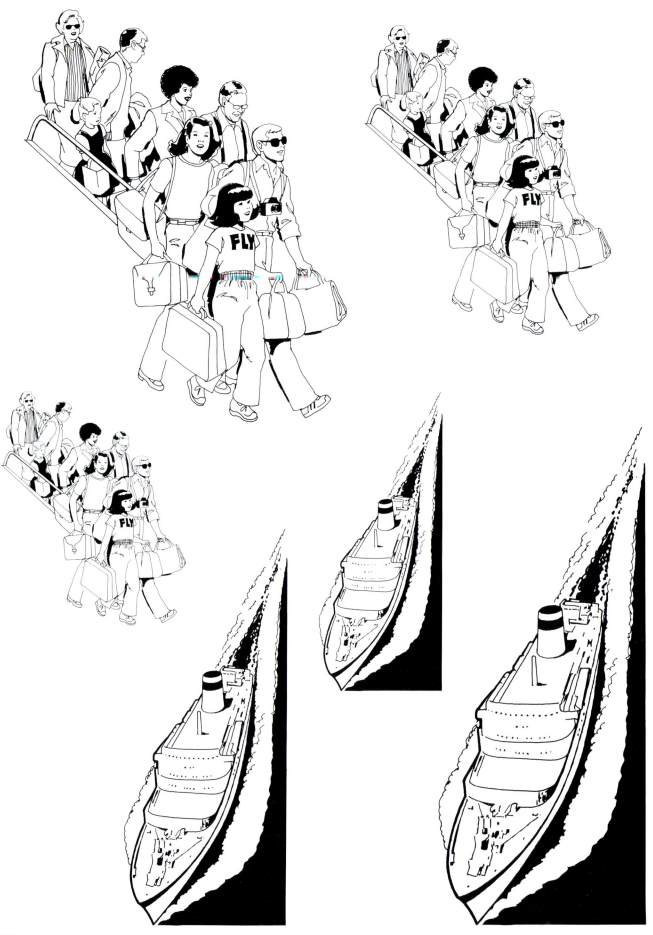

Caribbean

London

Andes

Japan

Mt. Rushmore

Amsterdam

Canada

Hawaii

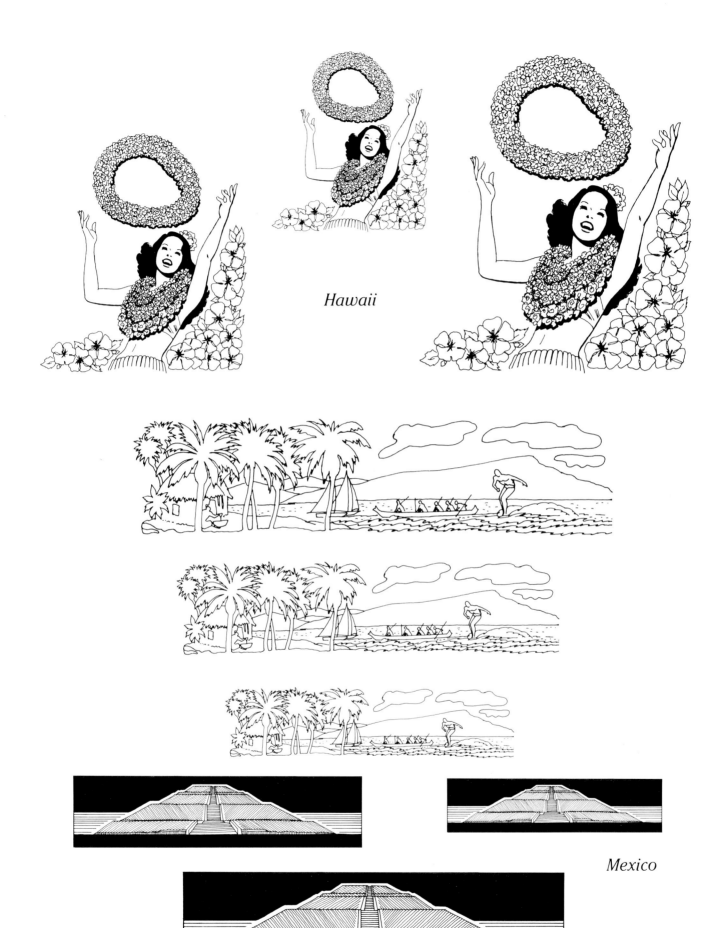

Hawaii

Mexico

Philadelphia

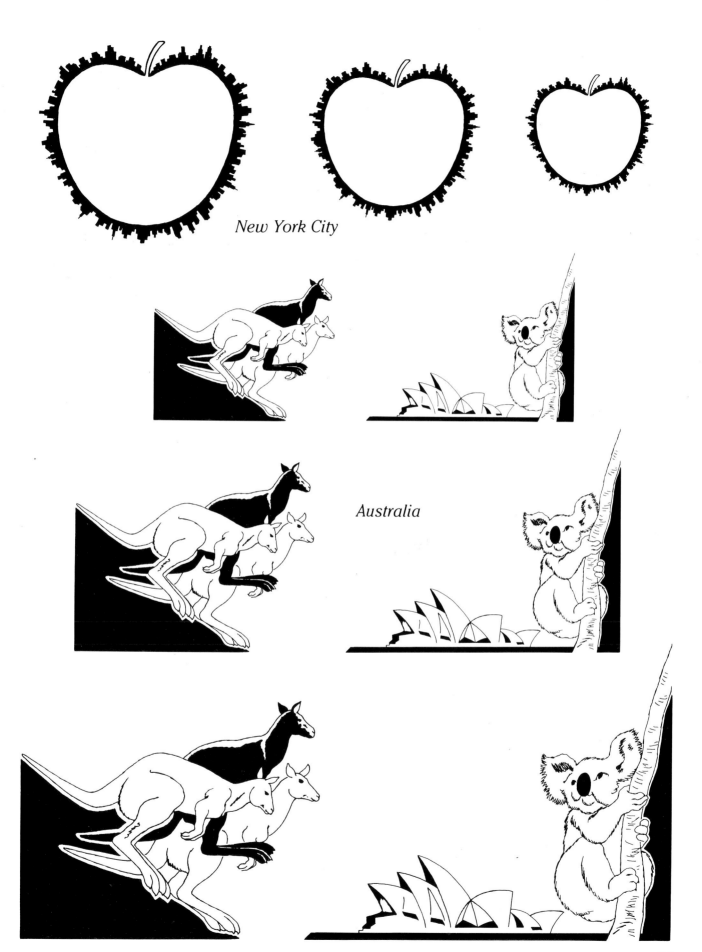